LEADERSHIP AND MANAGEMENT

TABLE OF CONTENTS

INTRODUCTION TO LEADERSHIP

OVERVIEW

Leadership is often defined as a process wherein an individual, influences and encourages others to achieve the organizational objectives and directs the organization so that it becomes more coherent and cohesive to work.
Moreover, a person who can bring out the change is the one who possesses the ability to be a leader. A good leader is one who always looks out for others before himself and is proactive. Proactive refers to a leader's tendency to be three steps ahead of others, thinking of all the possibilities of a scenario. Leadership is all about developing people and, in turn helping them to reach their maximum potential. In the simplest of terms, Leadership is the art of motivating people to help achieve a common goal.

1. INTRODUCTION TO LEADERSHIP

1.1 INTRODUCTION

Leadership is a complex and dynamic concept that plays a crucial role in guiding individuals, teams, and organizations toward achieving common goals. It involves influencing, motivating, and directing others to work collaboratively and efficiently. Leadership is not confined to formal positions of authority but can be displayed by individuals at various levels and in diverse contexts.

Leadership is the ability of an individual or a group of people to influence and guide followers or members of an organization, society, or team. Leadership often is an attribute tied to a person's title, seniority, or ranking in a hierarchy. However, it's an attribute anyone can have or attain, even those without leadership positions. It's a developable skill that can be improved over time.

Leaders play vital roles in various sectors of society, spanning business, politics, religion, and social or community-based organizations. These individuals are recognized for their ability to make prudent and occasionally challenging decisions. They excel in articulating a well-defined vision, setting realistic goals, and equipping followers with the essential knowledge and tools required to attain those objectives.

1.1.1 Why is leadership important?

Leadership assumes a pivotal role in shaping the success and trajectory of a business. The efficacy of organizations relies on adept leaders who can effectively communicate the mission, vision, and goals, rallying team members around these objectives and ultimately realizing them. These skills become particularly crucial during times of crisis.

The prosperity and evolution of a business often hinge on the ability to make challenging decisions. Successful leaders in businesses possess high competencies and emotional intelligence, enabling them to navigate tough choices and solve problems. This fosters a level of trust and accomplishment that cultivates positive, productive work environments, fostering teamwork, employee well-being, and robust work cultures that are appealing to top talent.

In the realm of organizational competitiveness, robust leadership is indispensable as it propels change and innovation. Astute leaders monitor shifts in their industry, champion novel ideas from within their company, and welcome innovative thinkers, thereby contributing to the organization's adaptability and forward-thinking approach.

1.2 MANAGEMENT

Management is all about performing pre-planned tasks regularly with the help of subordinates. A manager is completely responsible for carrying out the four important functions of management: planning, organizing, leading, and controlling. Managers can only become leaders if they adequately carry out leadership responsibilities, including communication of good and bad, providing inspiration and guidance, and encouraging employees to rise to a higher level of productivity.

1.2.1 The Difference Between Leadership and Management

While it's possible to be a good manager and leader at the same time, being decent at one doesn't necessarily mean you'll be proficient at the other. In this section, we'll examine the main differences between leadership and management.

1. **Creating visions vs executing ideas:** When it comes to implementing an organization's vision, leaders and managers take slightly different approaches. Leaders are more visionary and aim to inspire colleagues in terms of how they act and fulfill company goals. Alternatively, managers will monitor how their team is performing and whether they're adhering to an organization's vision.

   Put simply, good leadership focuses on the creation of sharing ideas in an engaging and inspiring way, whereas good management will make sure those ideas are being executed efficiently. Rather than looking at what task to accomplish, a manager will focus on the details of how to accomplish it. This will be done by delegating responsibilities to colleagues.

2. **Aligning vs organizing:** A key part of leadership is to influence how people contribute to company goals, ensuring everybody is aligned and on the same page. It's then down to management to break down these goals and organize resources effectively so that they can be achieved. A manager's approach is a lot more coordinated and technical.

   While a manager tends to be more focused on the details, a leader is expected to look at the bigger picture and apply a wider context to the way they think. If they're able to ensure the whole organization is aligned in terms of objectives, then managers can focus on their teams to ensure they're pulling in the same direction.

3. **Shaping culture vs day-to-day management:** The final difference in the leader vs manager debate is that good leaders tend to focus on the future, whereas competent managers will be more present-focused.
   Managers focus on plans, strategies, budgets, and responsibilities to ensure both themselves and their colleagues meet wider company objectives. However, leaders will aim to shape company culture by conjuring up future initiatives and possible growth opportunities.
   While leaders will aim to inspire employees to follow their example, managers will be responsible for holding staff members responsible if they don't follow the company culture set out by the leadership team. They'll fulfill this duty by monitoring employee progress and tracking day-to-day work activity.

1.2.2 Importance of Leadership in Management:

The importance of leadership in any group activity is too obvious to be over-emphasized. Wherever there is an organized group of people working towards a common goal, some type of leadership becomes essential. Lawrence A. Appley remarked that the time had come to substitute the word leadership for management.

Although the concern for leadership is as old as recorded history, it has become more acute during the last few decades due to the complexities of production methods, the high degree of specialization, and social changes in modern organizations. A good dynamic leader is compared to a 'dynamo generating energy' that charges and activates the entire group in such a way that near miracles may be achieved. The success of an enterprise depends to a great extent, upon effective leadership.'

The importance of leadership is the following:

1. **It Improves Motivation and Morale**: Through dynamic leadership, managers can improve the motivation and morale of their subordinates. A good leader influences the behavior of an individual in such a manner that he voluntarily works towards the achievement of enterprise goals.

2. **It Acts as a Motive Power to Group Efforts**: Leadership serves as a motive power for group efforts. It leads the group to a higher level of performance through its persistent efforts and impact on human relations.

3. **It Acts as an Aid to Authority:** The use of authority alone cannot always bring the desired results. Leadership acts as an aid to authority by influencing, inspiring, and initiating action.

4. **It is Needed at All Levels of Management:** Leadership plays a pivotal role at all levels of management because, in the absence of effective leadership, no management can achieve the desired results.

5. **It Rectifies the Imperfectness of the Formal Organisational Relationships**: No organizational structure can provide all types of relationships and people with common interests may work beyond the confines of formal relationships. Such informal relationships are more effective in controlling and regulating the behaviour of subordinates. Effective leadership uses their informal relationships to accomplish the enterprise goals.

6. **It Provides the Basis for Cooperation:** Effective leadership increases the understanding between the subordinates and the management and promotes cooperation among them.

1.2.3 Nature and Characteristics of Leadership:

An analysis of the definitions cited above reveals the following important characteristics of leadership:

1. Leadership is a personal quality.
2. It exists only with followers. If there are no followers, there is no leadership.
3. It is the willingness of people to follow that makes a person a leader.
4. Leadership is a process of influence. A leader must be able to influence the behaviour, attitude, and beliefs of his subordinates.
5. It exists only for the realization of common goals.
6. It involves a readiness to accept complete responsibility in all situations.

7. Leadership is the function of stimulating the followers to strive willingly to attain organizational objectives.
8. Leadership styles do change under different circumstances.
9. Leadership is neither bossism nor synonymous with; management.

1.3 HISTORICAL PERSPECTIVES ON LEADERSHIP

Historical perspectives on leadership have evolved, shaped by cultural, social, and political contexts. Different eras and civilizations have valued and conceptualized leadership in diverse ways. Here are some key historical perspectives on leadership:

a) **Ancient Civilizations:** In ancient civilizations such as Egypt, Mesopotamia, and Greece, leadership was often associated with divine authority. Pharaohs, kings, and rulers were considered gods or chosen by gods to lead.
   Greek philosophers like Plato and Aristotle explored the idea of the "philosopher-king" and the virtues associated with effective leadership, emphasizing wisdom, justice, and courage.
b) **Feudalism and Monarchies:** During the feudal era, leadership was often based on hereditary nobility. Kings and monarchs ruled by divine right and leadership was tied to lineage.
   Machiavelli's work in the Renaissance, particularly "The Prince," provided a pragmatic perspective on leadership, emphasizing political realism and the need for leaders to make tough decisions.
c) **Industrial Revolution:** The Industrial Revolution marked a shift in leadership models, with the rise of industrial and business leaders. Leadership became associated with managerial skills and efficiency.
   Max Weber introduced the concept of bureaucratic leadership, emphasizing rationality, hierarchy, and rules.
d) **Transformational Leadership:** In the 20th century, scholars like James MacGregor Burns and Bernard Bass introduced the concept of transformational leadership. This approach focuses on inspiring and motivating followers to achieve beyond their self-interests.
e) Mahatma Gandhi and Martin Luther King Jr. are often cited as transformational leaders who brought about social change through nonviolent means.
f) **Contingency and Situational Leadership:** Leadership theories in the mid-20th century, such as those by Fred Fiedler and Ken Blanchard, introduced contingency and situational perspectives. These theories suggest that effective leadership depends on the situation, and different styles may be suitable in different contexts.
g) **Modern Leadership Theories:** Contemporary leadership theories, including servant leadership, authentic leadership, and adaptive leadership, emphasize the importance of ethical conduct, authenticity, and adaptability in leadership roles.

h) **Globalization and Diversity:** In the 21st century, leadership perspectives have expanded to consider the challenges of a globalized world and diverse workplaces. Leaders are expected to navigate cultural differences and promote inclusivity.

i) **Digital Age Leadership:** With the advent of the digital age, leadership has evolved to address the challenges and opportunities presented by technology. Leaders are expected to be tech-savvy, adaptable to change, and capable of leading in virtual environments.

Overall, historical perspectives on leadership reflect the dynamic nature of societal values, organizational structures, and the understanding of effective leadership qualities across different epochs. Leadership theories continue to adapt to the changing landscape of the world and the expectations placed on leaders in various domains.

1.3.1 Leadership Traits

Leadership traits refer to the specific qualities or characteristics that individuals possess and that contribute to their effectiveness as leaders. These traits are personal attributes that influence how individuals lead, motivate, and guide others. Over the years, researchers and scholars have identified various leadership traits that are commonly associated with successful leaders. While there is no universal set of traits that guarantee effective leadership in all situations, certain qualities tend to be recognized as important for leadership success.

Leadership traits can encompass a wide range of attributes, including personal, interpersonal, and cognitive qualities. Some commonly recognized leadership traits include self-confidence, integrity, vision, initiative, adaptability, resilience, empathy, communication skills, decisiveness, influence, accountability, courage, strategic thinking, humility, and charisma.

It's essential to note that effective leadership is not solely determined by possessing a checklist of traits. The context, the nature of the organization or group being led, and the specific challenges at hand all influence the relevance and importance of different traits. Additionally, leadership is a dynamic and evolving skill, and individuals can develop and enhance their leadership traits over time through learning and experience.

In summary, leadership traits are the inherent characteristics that contribute to a person's ability to lead and influence others positively. Understanding and cultivating these traits can contribute to effective leadership in various settings and circumstances.

1.3.2 Qualities and Characteristics of Leadership Traits

Leadership traits encompass a set of personal qualities and characteristics that contribute to effective leadership. While there is no one-size-fits-all list of traits, as leadership is context-dependent, several common characteristics are often associated with successful leaders. Here are some key characteristics of leadership traits:

1) **Self-Confidence:** Confident leaders inspire trust and assurance in their team. They believe in their abilities and can make decisions with conviction.

2) **Integrity:** Leaders with integrity are honest, ethical, and principled. They prioritize transparency and adhere to a strong moral code.
3) **Vision:** Successful leaders have a clear vision of the future and can communicate it effectively to their team. They inspire others with a compelling sense of purpose.
4) **Initiative:** Leaders are proactive and take the initiative. They don't wait for problems to arise but rather anticipate challenges and take action.
5) **Adaptability:** In a rapidly changing environment, leaders must be adaptable. They can adjust strategies and plans to meet evolving circumstances.

6) **Resilience:** Resilient leaders bounce back from setbacks. They maintain composure under pressure and remain steadfast in pursuing goals.

7) **Empathy:** Empathetic leaders understand and share the feelings of others. They can relate to their team members and foster a positive work environment.

8) **Communication Skills:** Leaders must be effective communicators. This includes the ability to articulate ideas clearly, actively listen, and foster open dialogue within the team.

9) **Decisiveness:** Decisive leaders can make tough decisions promptly. They weigh available information and take decisive action when needed.

10) **Influence:** Leaders can influence and inspire others. They can motivate their team and gain commitment to shared goals.

11) **Accountability:** Accountable leaders take responsibility for their actions and the outcomes of their decisions. They set high standards for themselves and their team.

12) **Courage:** Courageous leaders are not afraid to take risks or challenge the status quo. They demonstrate moral and physical courage in their decisions.

13) **Strategic Thinking:** Leaders with strategic thinking can analyze complex situations, anticipate future trends, and develop long-term plans to achieve organizational objectives.

14) **Humility:** Humble leaders acknowledge the contributions of their team and are open to feedback. They create a collaborative and inclusive work environment.

15) **Charisma:** Charismatic leaders have a magnetic presence that attracts and inspires others. They create enthusiasm and a positive organizational culture.

These leadership traits are interconnected and often complement each other. Effective leaders possess a combination of these characteristics and can adapt their approach based on the specific needs of their team and the challenges they face. Leadership is a dynamic and evolving skill, and individuals can develop and enhance these traits through self-awareness, learning, and experience.

CONCLUSION

Leadership is a complex notion that includes a diverse range of skills, values, and traits. It extends beyond mere titles and authority, encompassing the capacity to inspire, motivate, and steer others toward a shared objective. Proficient leaders exhibit attributes like integrity, adaptability, resilience, collaboration, ongoing learning, empathy, and emotional intelligence. They establish a constructive and inclusive atmosphere that nurtures trust, loyalty, and exceptional performance. Leadership isn't confined to a privileged few; rather, it is a skill that can be nurtured and honed by anyone ready to embrace the responsibilities and hurdles that accompany it.

EXERCISES

1. How does leadership contribute to the development of talent and the succession planning process?
2. What is the role of leadership in fostering diversity, equity, and inclusion within a workplace?
3. How can leadership positively influence the alignment of individual and organizational goals?
4. What are some key leadership traits that you believe are essential for success in a leadership role, and how have you personally developed or leveraged these traits in your leadership journey?
5. Describe the main characteristics of a Leadership trait.
6. Explain the difference between Leadership and Management.

2. LEADERSHIP THEORIES & STYLES

TABLE OF CONTENTS

LEADERSHIP THEORIES & STYLES

OVERVIEW

Leadership theories seek to elucidate the processes through which individuals ascend to leadership positions, delving into the reasons behind their emergence as leaders. These theories concentrate on identifying the traits and behaviors that individuals can cultivate to enhance their leadership prowess. Among the key attributes emphasized by leaders as crucial for effective leadership are unwavering ethics and elevated moral standards.

A leadership style denotes the approach employed by a leader to achieve the team's objectives, primarily by inspiring employees to contribute towards shared goals while prioritizing their well-being. A profound comprehension of leadership styles is essential for fostering cohesive teamwork and continual growth, especially in the face of evolving circumstances.

2. INTRODUCTION

In the realm of leadership, numerous theories explore the dynamics of leadership, the qualities of effective leaders, and strategies for achieving success. Managers can adopt various leadership styles, and the influence of these styles depends on factors such as the specific group they lead and the industry they operate in. These leadership theories elucidate the workings of different leadership styles within a company, contributing to its success. For those aspiring to become business leaders or managers, a comprehensive understanding of these diverse leadership theories is crucial to navigating and shaping their own leadership and management approach.

Leadership theories are the explanations of how and why certain people become leaders. They focus on the traits and behaviors that people can adopt to increase their leadership capabilities. Some of the top traits that leaders say are vital to good leadership include:

- Strong ethics and high moral standards
- Great self-organizational skills
- Efficient learner
- Nurtures growth in employees
- Fosters connection and belonging

Studies indicate that certain traits are universally regarded as crucial for leaders worldwide. Leadership theories play a key role in elucidating how leaders leverage and cultivate these traits. In recent times, there has been a trend toward greater formalization of leadership theories, rendering them more accessible for comprehension, discussion, and practical analysis.

Ralph Nader articulates a perspective on leadership, asserting, "The function of leadership is to produce more leaders, not followers." This notion aligns with the concept of transformational leadership, where a leader can reshape a follower's perspective or psychology, instilling in them the desire to become leaders themselves. This underscores the belief that, ultimately, leadership should be uplifting and inspirational. Leaders are tasked with propelling those they lead to new heights, fostering their growth into their full potential.

Understanding transformational leadership is paramount for leaders aspiring to genuinely influence and impact others. Various leadership theories aim to fortify and enhance leadership, encouraging followers to aspire to leadership roles themselves.

2.1 DIFFERENT LEADERSHIP THEORIES

While there are dozens of leadership theories and psychology, there are a few that are more well-known. These more common leadership theories are important to understand and recognize. Understanding the psychological and social impacts of effective leadership will help to determine the kind of leader one's wants to be.

2.1.1 Behavioral Theory

The behavioral leadership theory centers on the actions of leaders, positing that these behaviors can be emulated by other leaders. Also known as the style theory, it contends that successful leaders are not inherently born but can be developed through learnable behavior. Behavioral leadership theories emphasize the conduct of a leader, asserting that the most reliable predictor of leadership success lies in observing a leader's actions. Behavioral learning theory emphasizes actions rather than inherent qualities, categorizing observed patterns of behavior into various "styles of leadership." These styles include task-oriented leaders, people-oriented leaders, country club leaders, status-quo leaders, dictatorial leaders, and more. Ultimately, in this theory, the measure of success lies in a leader's actual behaviors and actions.

The behavioral theory offers several advantages, notably the belief that leaders can learn and consciously choose actions to mold themselves into the desired type of leader. It promotes flexibility, allowing leaders to adapt to different circumstances. Moreover, it suggests that anyone has the potential to become a leader. However, drawbacks include the lack of specific guidance on how to behave in particular situations, as the theory encompasses numerous leadership styles without a universally applicable one.

A practical illustration of the behavioral theory can be seen in the comparison between a task-oriented leader and a people-oriented leader. When faced with team issues, a task-oriented leader evaluates the process and workflow, seeking adjustments. On the other hand, a people-oriented leader directly approaches individuals, inquiring about the root cause of the problem. Regardless of the chosen behaviors, the behavioral leadership theory encourages leaders to focus on their actions and use their decisions to cultivate effective leadership.

2.1.2 Contingency Theory

The contingency leadership theory, also known as Situational Theory, directs attention to the contextual aspects surrounding a leader. These theories examine how the success or failure of a leader is influenced by the specific situation. The effectiveness of a leader is intricately tied to the situational context, with a leader's personality playing a minor role in comparison. According to this theory, leaders can adapt their leadership styles based on situational demands, and it proposes that matching the right leader to a specific situation may be optimal. Examples of contingency theories encompass Hershey and Blanchard's Situational Theory, Evans and House's Path-Goal Theory, and Fiedler's Contingency Theory.

Contingency theory boasts notable advantages, particularly the idea that leaders can achieve effectiveness irrespective of their situational context. However, it faces criticism for lacking sufficient detail in contextual analysis. While emphasizing the importance of the situation, it may not adequately consider the psychological aspects of employees or the company itself. Furthermore, it might not sufficiently address the potential evolution of leadership styles over time.

Leaders and their situations are influenced by both internal and external factors. Internal factors include the type of company, team size, and an individual's inherent leadership style, while external factors may involve customer sentiments and market conditions. All these elements contribute to the nuances of the contingency theory.

2.1.3 Great Man Theory

The leadership concept known as the Great Man Theory also referred to as the Trait Theory, posits that effective leaders are inherently born with specific traits and skills that set them apart, qualities that cannot be acquired through teaching or learning. According to this theory, individuals attain leadership positions due to their unique inherent attributes. However, the Trait Theory faces considerable criticism, primarily centered around the notion that leadership is predetermined – one is either born a leader or not, without the need for effort or development. This implies that social and psychological leaders are predestined and cannot emerge from obscurity; they are either selected or not. Additionally, critics argue that many traits associated with this theory are inherently masculine and do not accurately reflect the diverse psychological makeup of effective leaders.

Historical figures like Abraham Lincoln, Alexander the Great, and Queen Elizabeth I are often cited as examples of the Great Man Theory, as they utilized their exceptional skills to lead nations. The theory suggests that leaders who embody its principles, displaying high levels of ambition and determination, tend to rise to prominence. In contemporary times, leaders ascending to the top may perceive their traits and abilities as aligning with the "great man" theory, reinforcing the notion that leadership positions are attained based on inherent gifts.

2.1.4 Participative Theory

Participative leadership, also known as democratic leadership, is not as prevalent in the corporate world. This leadership approach advocates for direct employee involvement in organizational decision-making processes. The leader's role is to facilitate discussions, gather suggestions, and formulate the best possible course of action. In this model, everyone actively contributes to decisions for the team and organization, with the leader guiding rather than dictating.

While there are several advantages to this approach, such as increased employee engagement and motivation through direct involvement in decisions, it is not without criticism. Some argue that participative leadership may make leaders appear weak or unnecessary. Additionally, critics contend that leaders following this style might prioritize individual preferences over the company's overall needs, potentially leading to suboptimal outcomes.

A notable example of participative leadership is Bill Gates. Although this leadership theory remains a topic of debate, numerous companies strive to integrate employees more into the decision-making process. In this model, leaders may conduct meetings to seek employee input on solving specific problems, encouraging open and honest communication. After collecting suggestions, leaders collaborate with their peers to make decisions based on both employee input and their judgment. While employees often appreciate this leadership style, it may be perceived as less effective overall.

2.1.5 Transactional Leadership

Transactional leadership is a leadership approach centered on organization, performance, and supervision, utilizing a system of rewards and punishments to maintain employee motivation. This style relies on two primary mechanisms: rewards and punishments. For instance, if an employee successfully achieves a predetermined goal, the organization will provide them with rewards. Conversely, failure to meet the set objectives results in consequences.

Transactional leaders can be categorized as either active or passive. Active transactional leaders actively monitor and assess employee performance. In contrast, passive leaders concentrate solely on the target, checking for fulfillment and addressing issues after the task is completed. Transactional leadership is well-suited for situations where strict adherence to rules is necessary, and there is limited room for creativity or innovation.

a) The Benefits of Transactional Leadership

Transactional leadership offers several valuable advantages that contribute to the development of an efficient team. Below are the benefits associated with transactional leadership:

1) **Promotes Equity:** Transactional leaders employ a system of rewards and penalties to motivate employees, ensuring that everyone is treated fairly. Performance determines rewards, eliminating any bias based on the leader's personal opinions, and fostering an environment free from favoritism or partiality.
2) **Straightforward Leadership Style:** The transactional leadership model is easily understandable. Employees are aware that achieving set targets within a

specified timeframe leads to rewards, while failure incurs consequences. This simplicity helps maintain a focused approach to tasks.

3) **Clarity on Impact**: Employees, by meeting organizational goals, can directly observe the positive outcomes of their hard work. This realization not only serves as inspiration but also provides a profound sense of satisfaction among employees.

b) Disadvantages:

While transactional leadership comes with several advantages, it also carries certain drawbacks. These are outlined below:

1) **Lack of Emphasis on Relationship Building:** Transactional leaders prioritize supervising whether employees meet targets over fostering relationships. The focus on rewards or punishments based on performance may inspire followers, but the downside is neglect of efforts to create a positive work environment. This deficiency makes it challenging for both followers and leaders to establish healthy relationships.
2) **Difficulty in Choosing Appropriate Rewards:** Each individual has unique needs and preferences, ranging from a desire for monetary rewards to time off or a promotion. Identifying a reward that satisfies all employees becomes a daunting task. Consequently, many organizations encounter challenges when implementing a transactional leadership system.
3) **Constraints on Creativity:** Transactional leadership, being goal-oriented, setting specific targets for followers to achieve within a defined timeframe. However, this structured approach leaves little room for creativity or innovation. Employees are bound by the established framework, limiting opportunities for them to apply their problem-solving methods and stifling innovation within the organization.

2.1.6 Transformational Leadership

Transformational leadership involves leaders inspiring and motivating their followers to achieve optimal performance. Through motivation, leaders aim to elicit the best efforts from their followers. In this approach, the leader serves as a role model and establishes a vision or goal for the entire organization. Additionally, transformational leaders inspire their followers to enhance their abilities and skills while providing support in cultivating self-confidence.

a) Characteristics of Transformational Leadership

Transformational leadership encompasses four key characteristics:

1) **Personalized Consideration:** Leaders prioritize the needs and requirements of their followers, demonstrating support and empathy. Each follower receives individualized attention, fostering trust between the organization and its employees.
2) **Inspirational Motivation**: Leaders motivate and inspire followers by presenting a compelling vision. To achieve a goal, followers must have a sense of purpose, and leaders play a crucial role in making the vision both understandable and motivating. This serves as an effective tool for instilling a collective sense of purpose.
3) **Personalized Inspiration:** In transformational leadership, the leader serves as a role model, embodying the skills, knowledge, and qualities desired in their followers. By representing core values and trust, leaders make it easier for followers to place trust in them and feel inspired to emulate their leadership qualities.
4) **Intellectual Stimulation**: Leaders encourage followers to think creatively and innovatively. They inspire and support followers to explore beyond conventional boundaries, fostering a culture that encourages trying new things.

b) Advantages of Transformational Leadership

Transformational leadership proves effective due to several key benefits:

1) **Fosters Motivation**: Transformational leaders prioritize employee motivation and encouragement, taking the time to understand each employee as an individual. Building strong relationships with followers inspires and motivates them to give their best, contributing to the organization's growth.
2) **Cultivates Loyalty and Reduces Employee Turnover**: Through open communication and making employees feel valued, transformational leaders establish a sense of belonging within the organization. When employees perceive recognition and value in their work, they develop loyalty, resulting in a positive impact on reducing employee turnover.

3) **Supports Professional Development**: Transformational leaders guide members in achieving organizational goals and actively promote their professional development. This involves encouraging the enhancement of skills to advance careers. Such support from leaders significantly contributes to employee development, fostering competence and confidence and playing a pivotal role in personal and professional growth.
4) **Facilitates Smooth Transitions:** Transformational leadership employs effective change management techniques. Leaders prepare employees for environmental changes, guiding them through transitions seamlessly and without encountering difficulties. This proactive approach ensures a smooth adaptation to new circumstances.

In addition, a transformational leader supports the employees throughout the process. They do it by creating a system or helping them find the right direction. Also, sometimes they may do so by providing additional flexibility to the employees for coping with the change.

c) Disadvantages of Transformational Leadership

1) **Requires Continuous Communication:** Sustaining effective communication with each team member is a crucial demand placed on the leader. This task can be overwhelming, particularly when leaders juggle multiple responsibilities. The challenge intensifies in larger teams, turning the entire communication process into a time-consuming and exhausting endeavor for the leader.
2) **Not Appropriate for Short-Term Goals:** The transformational leadership system excels in achieving long-term objectives. Consequently, when an organization seeks rapid goal accomplishment, this leadership approach may prove less effective.
3) **Prolonged Decision-Making Process:** The emphasis on valuing every opinion within transformational leadership can sometimes impede the decision-making process. Gathering feedback from all employees before reaching a decision may not be practical in every situation. Therefore, effective leaders discern when to make decisions on behalf of the team and when to solicit feedback to inform their choices.

Leadership is a complex undertaking. To excel as a leader, one must comprehend the needs of their followers and employ leadership styles tailored to them. This necessitates the ability to distinguish between transactional and transformational leadership, understanding when each is most appropriate.

2.2 LEADERSHIP STYLES

Leadership styles encompass the behavioral approach that leaders employ to influence, motivate, and guide their followers. These styles dictate how leaders execute plans and strategies to achieve specific objectives, taking into consideration stakeholder expectations and the well-being of their team.

Various forums have extensively examined leadership styles to identify the most appropriate or effective approach that inspires and guides others toward goal attainment. The fundamental aspect of an effective leadership style lies in its ability to foster follower trust.

Research studies suggest that followers who trust their leader are more likely to adhere to the leader's instructions beyond expectations. Consequently, they tend to achieve established goals while also feeling empowered to express their ideas and suggestions freely regarding the direction of ongoing projects.

Common Leadership Styles

2.2.1 Democratic Leadership

A leadership style characterized as democratic involves the leader making decisions based on input from team members. This collaborative and consultative approach allows each team member to contribute to the direction of ongoing projects, although the ultimate responsibility for decision-making lies with the leader.

Widely recognized as one of the most popular and effective leadership styles, democratic leadership empowers lower-level employees by providing them a voice, making it crucial within organizations. This style mirrors decision-making processes observed in company boardrooms and may involve voting to reach decisions.

In addition to decision-making, democratic leadership entails the delegation of authority, allowing others to determine work assignments. This approach leverages the skills and experiences of team members in task execution. The democratic leadership style fosters creativity and engagement, often resulting in high job satisfaction and increased productivity. However, reaching a consensus among team members can be time-consuming and costly, particularly when swift decisions are required.

Also known as participative leadership, democratic leadership actively involves team members in decision-making processes, offering numerous advantages alongside certain disadvantages.

Here are the advantages and disadvantages of democratic leadership:

a) Advantages of Democratic Leadership:

- **Increased employee engagement**: By involving team members in decision-making, democratic leadership increases their sense of ownership and engagement. When employees feel their opinions are valued, they become more committed to the organization's goals and objectives.
- **Enhanced creativity and innovation**: Democratic leadership encourages the sharing of ideas and diverse perspectives. This fosters a culture of creativity and innovation, as team members feel empowered to contribute their unique insights and suggestions.
- **Higher job satisfaction and motivation:** When employees have a voice in decision-making, they tend to feel more satisfied and motivated. They are more likely to take pride in their work and demonstrate a higher level of commitment and dedication.
- **Better problem-solving:** In democratic leadership, decisions are made through collective input and deliberation. This allows for a broader range of viewpoints and ideas, leading to better problem-solving and decision-making outcomes.
- **Development of leadership skills**: By involving team members in the decision-making process, democratic leadership helps in developing their leadership skills. It cultivates a culture of leadership development, empowering individuals to take initiative and make informed decisions.

b) Disadvantages of Democratic Leadership:

- **Time-consuming:** Democratic leadership involves gathering input and reaching a consensus, which can be time-consuming. This style of decision-making may not be suitable for situations that require quick decisions or during emergencies.
- **Lack of efficiency:** The involvement of multiple individuals in decision-making can slow down the decision-making process and lead to inefficiencies. The need for consensus may result in compromises that may not always yield the most effective or efficient outcomes.
- **Potential for conflicts:** When different team members with diverse opinions and perspectives participate in decision-making, conflicts may arise. Disagreements and disputes can slow down progress and hinder the decision-making process.
- **Decision paralysis**: In some cases, the involvement of too many people in decision-making can lead to decision paralysis. If consensus cannot be reached or if too much time is spent deliberating, decisions may be delayed or even avoided altogether.
- **Inequality of input:** In a democratic leadership style, not all team members may have equal influence or assertiveness to voice their opinions. This can result in the dominance of a few individuals, while others may feel marginalized or unheard.

It's important to note that the effectiveness of democratic leadership depends on various factors such as the nature of the task, the maturity and expertise of the team members, and the organizational context. Different leadership styles may be more appropriate in different situations, and leaders may need to adapt their approach accordingly.

2.2.2 Autocratic Leadership

Autocratic leadership stands in stark contrast to democratic leadership. In this style, the leader unilaterally makes all decisions on behalf of the team without seeking input or suggestions from its members. The leader assumes full authority and responsibility, wielding absolute power and directing all tasks without employee consultation. Following the decision-making process, everyone is expected to support the leader's decision, often accompanied by a level of fear within the team.

The autocratic leadership style can be regressive, fostering employee dissatisfaction as decisions may not align with their interests. For example, a leader might impose unilateral increases in working hours or unfavorable changes in other working conditions to boost production, without considering employee input. This lack of consultation can lead to the manager being unaware of the reasons behind stagnant production, resorting to forced increases in working hours and subsequently causing persistent absenteeism and high employee turnover.

Nevertheless, autocratic leadership can prove effective when the leader possesses experience and knowledge relevant to the decision at hand, especially in situations where swift decision-making is essential. There are instances where this approach is deemed appropriate, such as when a decision doesn't require team input or agreement for a successful outcome.

a) Merits of Autocratic Leadership:

- **Quick Decision-Making**: Autocratic leaders can make decisions quickly without wasting time discussing with others. This helps in taking immediate action when needed.
- **Clear Direction**: Autocratic leaders give clear instructions and goals to their team members. This helps everyone know what needs to be done, which can improve efficiency.
- **Maintaining Order and Discipline**: Autocratic leaders ensure that rules are followed and maintain a disciplined work environment, which can be important for safety and precision in certain jobs.

b) Demerits of Autocratic Leadership:

- **Lack of Employee Involvement:** Autocratic leaders make decisions without asking for input from their team members. This can make employees feel undervalued and demotivated, leading to lower job satisfaction.

- **Limited Innovation:** Autocratic leaders don't often consider new ideas or suggestions from their team. This can discourage creativity and innovation, as employees may hesitate to share their thoughts.
- **Dependency on the Leader**: Autocratic leaders make all the decisions, which can create a reliance on them. This can prevent team members from developing their skills and decision-making abilities.
- **Lack of Flexibility**: Autocratic leaders may struggle to adapt to changing situations or consider different viewpoints. This rigidity can make it difficult for the team to respond to new challenges or seize opportunities.

2.2.3 Laissez-Faire Leadership

Laissez-faire leadership is accurately characterized as a hands-off or passive approach to leading. In this style, leaders furnish their team members with the necessary tools, information, and resources for executing their work tasks. The essence of this leadership style, often expressed as "let them be," involves the leader stepping back and allowing team members to work without direct supervision, granting them the freedom to plan, organize, make decisions, address challenges, and complete assigned projects.

The laissez-faire leadership approach empowers employees who are creative, skilled, and self-motivated. Providing a high level of trust and independence to the team can contribute to increased morale, productivity, and job satisfaction.

However, it is crucial to exercise caution with this leadership style, as unchecked laissez-faire leadership may lead to chaos and confusion if the team lacks organization. Without proper guidance, team members might diverge from the leader's expectations and end up pursuing entirely different paths. Laissez-faire leadership is a hands-off approach where the leader grants subordinates a significant degree of autonomy and decision-making authority.

While this leadership style can have its merits, it also has its demerits. Let's explore both sides:

a) Merits of laissez-faire leadership:

- **Creativity and innovation:** By giving employees the freedom to make decisions and take ownership of their work, laissez-faire leadership can foster a culture of creativity and innovation. Employees are more likely to explore new ideas and find innovative solutions when they have the freedom to do so.
- **Employee empowerment:** Laissez-faire leadership empowers employees by allowing them to make decisions and take responsibility for their work. This can lead to higher levels of job satisfaction and motivation, as employees feel trusted and valued by their leader.
- **Flexibility and adaptability**: Laissez-faire leadership allows for greater flexibility and adaptability within an organization. Employees have the freedom to respond quickly to

changes and make decisions based on their expertise, which can be advantageous in fast-paced and dynamic environments.

b) **Demerits of laissez-faire leadership:**

- **Lack of structure and guidance**: One of the main drawbacks of laissez-faire leadership is the potential lack of structure and guidance. Without clear direction from a leader, employees may struggle to understand expectations and goals, leading to confusion and inefficiency.
- **Lack of accountability:** With a hands-off approach, laissez-faire leaders may not hold employees accountable for their actions and outcomes. This can result in a lack of discipline and a decline in productivity, as employees may not feel motivated to meet objectives or perform at their best.
- **Potential for decreased coordination:** Laissez-faire leadership may hinder coordination and collaboration within a team or organization. Without a leader actively overseeing and facilitating communication, employees may work in silos, leading to a lack of alignment and synergy among team members.
- **Increased risk of poor decision-making**: In some cases, laissez-faire leadership can lead to poor decision-making. Without the guidance and expertise of a leader, employees may make decisions that are not aligned with organizational goals or that lack a comprehensive understanding of the broader context.

It's worth noting that the effectiveness of laissez-faire leadership can vary depending on the specific situation and the capabilities of the individuals involved. In some cases, it can be a successful approach, while in others, it may lead to negative outcomes. Effective leadership often requires a flexible and adaptable approach that takes into account the needs of the organization and the individuals within it.

2.2.4 Servant Leadership

Servant leadership is a leadership approach where the leader prioritizes serving the team before assuming the role of a leader. In this model, a servant leader dedicates themselves to fulfilling the needs of their team ahead of their own. This leadership style is exemplified through leading by example, as servant leaders actively seek ways to foster the development, elevation, and inspiration of those following them, ultimately aiming for optimal results.

Effective implementation of servant leadership demands leaders with both high integrity and munificence. This approach contributes to the establishment of a positive organizational culture, fostering elevated morale among team members. Additionally, it cultivates an ethical environment characterized by robust values and ideals.

However, some scholars argue that servant leadership may not be well-suited for competitive scenarios where leaders are engaged in competition. In such situations, servant leaders might find themselves trailing behind more ambitious counterparts. Critics also contend that the servant leadership style may lack the agility needed to respond swiftly to tight deadlines and the rapid pace of high-velocity organizations or dynamic situations.

2.2.5 Charismatic Leadership

Charismatic leadership employs charisma to motivate and inspire followers. Leaders use eloquent communication skills to unite a team toward a shared vision. However, due to the charismatic leaders' overwhelming disposition, they can see themselves as bigger than the team and lose track of the important tasks.

2.2.6 Situational Leadership

This style involves adapting one's leadership approach based on the needs of the situation and the development level of the team members. It emphasizes flexibility and the ability to adjust leadership behaviors to best support the team.

Ultimately, effective leaders often demonstrate a blend of different leadership styles, adapting their approach based on the situation and the needs of their team. Leaders need to be flexible, self-aware, and able to assess the needs of their followers to determine which leadership style will be most effective in a given situation.

CONCLUSION

Numerous theories and styles exist in the realm of leadership, and even within these frameworks, various variables necessitate consideration. The exploration of different leaders' skills and tactics remains a captivating study, yet there is no singular, definitive approach to leadership. Certain qualities of exceptional leaders may be innate, while others are acquired through experiences, emphasizing the absence of a universal formula for greatness in leadership. Every situation presents unique challenges, requiring leaders to cultivate flexibility and hone analytical and communication skills for success in their roles.

EXERCISES

1. How do trait theories of leadership explain the characteristics that make an individual a successful leader?
2. In what ways do behavioral theories focus on the actions and behaviors of leaders rather than their inherent traits?
3. Can you elaborate on contingency theories and how they suggest that effective leadership depends on the specific situation?
4. What role do transformational leadership theories play in inspiring and motivating followers toward a shared vision?
5. How does a laissez-faire leadership style impact team dynamics and productivity, and when might it be suitable or unsuitable?
6. Can you provide examples of how a transformational leadership style has been successful in inspiring positive change within an organization?
7. What challenges might a leader face when adopting a servant leadership style, and how can these challenges be overcome?
8. How does a laissez-faire leadership style impact team dynamics and productivity, and when might it be suitable or unsuitable?

EMOTIONAL INTELLIGENCE

TABLE OF CONTENTS

OVERVIEW

Emotional intelligence (EI) is crucial for effective leadership, as it enables leaders to understand and manage their own emotions while influencing and connecting with others. It comprises self-awareness, self-regulation, motivation, empathy, and social skills. Leaders with high EI can stay composed under pressure, inspire and motivate teams, foster strong relationships, and handle conflicts with empathy and diplomacy. By creating a positive work environment and making well-informed decisions, emotionally intelligent leaders drive team performance and organizational success.

3.EMOTIONAL INTELLIGENCE

Emotional intelligence (EI or EQ for "emotional quotient") is the ability to perceive, interpret, demonstrate, control, evaluate, and use emotions to communicate with and relate to others effectively and constructively. This ability to express and control emotions is essential, but so is the ability to understand, interpret, and respond to the emotions of others. Some experts suggest that emotional intelligence is more important than IQ for success in life.

3.1 Components of Emotional Intelligence?

Researchers suggest that there are four different levels of emotional intelligence including emotional perception, the ability to reason using emotions, the ability to understand emotions, and the ability to manage emotions.

- **Perceiving emotions:** The first step in understanding emotions is to perceive them accurately. In many cases, this might involve understanding nonverbal signals such as body language and facial expressions.

- **Reasoning with emotions:** The next step involves using emotions to promote thinking and cognitive activity. Emotions help us prioritize what we pay attention to and react to; we respond emotionally to things that garner our attention.
- **Understanding emotions**: The emotions that we perceive can carry a wide variety of meanings. If someone is expressing angry emotions, the observer must interpret the cause of the person's anger and what it could mean. For example, if your boss is acting angry, it might mean that they are dissatisfied with your work, or it could be because they got a speeding ticket on their way to work that morning or that they've been fighting with their partner.
- **Managing emotions:** The ability to manage emotions effectively is a crucial part of emotional intelligence and the highest level. Regulating emotions and responding appropriately as well as responding to the emotions of others are all important aspects of emotional management.

The four branches of this model are arranged by complexity with the more basic processes at the lower levels and the more advanced processes at the higher levels. For example, the lowest levels involve perceiving and expressing emotion, while higher levels require greater conscious involvement and involve regulating emotions.

3.1.1 Emotional Intelligence For Strategic Leaders

Emotional intelligence for strategic leaders is the ability to understand, recognize, and manage one's own emotions and the emotions of others to make effective decisions and lead their organization.

Leaders with emotional intelligence can regulate their emotions, remain calm under pressure, and make rational decisions. They are also able to empathize with others, understand their perspectives and feelings, and communicate in a way that is empathetic and supportive.

Moreover, leaders with emotional intelligence can build positive relationships with employees, customers, and other stakeholders by understanding their needs, motivations, and emotions. They can create a work environment that is positive, engaging, and inclusive, leading to greater employee satisfaction, loyalty, and retention.

By incorporating emotional intelligence into their leadership style, strategic leaders can make decisions that take into account the emotional impact on those involved and lead their organization toward success. Overall, emotional intelligence is a critical skill for leaders who want to create a positive workplace culture, foster collaboration and innovation, and drive organizational growth.

3.1.2 Developing emotional intelligence skills

Emotional intelligence (EI) is a critical skill for effective leadership. EI refers to the ability to recognize, understand, and manage one's own emotions, as well as the emotions of others. Developing and increasing EI can help leaders improve their decision-making, communication, and interpersonal relationships. Here are some tips for increasing and developing emotional intelligence in leaders:

1. **Self-awareness:** Leaders should develop self-awareness, which is the ability to recognize and understand their own emotions. This involves reflecting on their feelings and reactions to situations, and understanding how their emotions affect their behavior and decision-making.
2. **Empathy:** Leaders should practice empathy, which is the ability to understand and recognize the emotions of others. This involves actively listening and understanding the perspectives of others and responding in a way that shows that their emotions are recognized and respected.
3. **Communication:** Leaders should develop effective communication skills to convey their emotions and understand the emotions of others. This includes active listening, nonverbal communication, and the ability to express emotions constructively and appropriately.
4. **Conflict resolution:** Leaders should learn effective conflict resolution techniques to manage disagreements and conflicts. This involves understanding the emotions and perspectives of others and finding a mutually beneficial solution.
5. **Self-regulation:** Leaders should practice self-regulation, which is the ability to control and manage their own emotions. This includes recognizing triggers, taking a pause before reacting and finding ways to manage emotions constructively.
6. **Continuous learning**: Leaders should always strive for continuous learning and personal growth. This includes seeking feedback, self-reflection, and seeking out learning opportunities to improve their emotional intelligence.

Increasing and developing emotional intelligence requires a conscious effort and a willingness to learn and grow. Leaders who prioritize emotional intelligence can improve their leadership effectiveness and build stronger relationships with their team mem.

3.1.3 How does emotional intelligence affect leaders in the workplace?

Emotional intelligence can have a significant impact on leaders in the workplace. Here are some ways it can affect them:

1. **Better decision-making:** Leaders with emotional intelligence can make better decisions because they can control their emotions and remain calm under pressure. They are also able to empathize with others and take their perspectives and emotions into account when making decisions.

2. **Improved communication:** Leaders with emotional intelligence can communicate effectively with their team members because they can read and understand emotions. They can communicate in a way that is clear, empathetic, and supportive, which can help build positive relationships with employees.
3. **Better collaboration:** Leaders with emotional intelligence can build strong relationships with their team members, which can lead to better collaboration and teamwork. They can listen to others, understand their perspectives, and work together to achieve common goals.
4. **Improved conflict resolution**: Leaders with emotional intelligence can manage conflict effectively because they can understand the emotions of others and communicate in a way that is empathetic and supportive. They can help to de-escalate conflict and find mutually beneficial solutions.
5. **Increased employee engagement:** Leaders with emotional intelligence can create a positive work environment that fosters employee engagement and loyalty. They can build trust with their team members, recognize and appreciate their contributions, and create a sense of purpose and meaning in the work that they do.

Overall, emotional intelligence can help leaders to be more effective in their roles by improving their decision-making, communication, collaboration, conflict resolution, and employee engagement.

EXERCISES

1. What is emotional intelligence (EI), and why is it important in leadership?
2. How does emotional intelligence differ from IQ in terms of success in life?
3. What are the key skills involved in emotional intelligence?
4. How can emotional intelligence help in building strong interpersonal relationships?
5. What are some real-life examples of emotional intelligence in action?
6. Why is reasoning with emotions important in decision-making?
7. How does understanding emotions help in interpreting others' feelings?
8. What role does managing emotions play in maintaining a positive work environment?

COMMUNICATION SKILLS FOR LEADERS

TABLE OF CONTENTS

OVERVIEW

Effective communication is a fundamental skill for leaders, enabling them to articulate their vision, build trust, and inspire teams toward shared goals. Strong leadership communication involves clarity, active listening, emotional intelligence, and adaptability. Leaders must convey messages concisely while also being open to feedback and different perspectives. Nonverbal cues, such as body language and tone, play a crucial role in ensuring alignment between words and intent. Additionally, the ability to provide constructive feedback, resolve conflicts, and motivate teams enhances workplace collaboration and productivity. Transparency and trust-building are essential, especially during times of change or crisis, where clear and reassuring communication keeps teams focused. By mastering these skills, leaders can foster a positive organizational culture, encourage innovation, and drive long-term success.

4. COMMUNICATION SKILLS FOR LEADERS

Effective communication is an essential leadership skill and a defining trait of a strong leader. Leaders must excel in conveying their message across various contexts and relationships—whether with individuals, organizations, communities or even on a global scale—to drive results through others.

Leadership communication is how leaders inform, inspire, and connect with others. It includes verbal, nonverbal, and written messages, covering everything from giving instructions and feedback to employees, sharing a vision, mediating conflicts within teams, and updating stakeholders. Effective communication is crucial for leadership success.

4.1 Why is Communication Important for Leaders?

Leaders must think, articulate ideas effectively, and share information with diverse audiences. They also need to manage the rapid flow of information within the organization and among colleagues, customers, partners, and vendors.

Strong leadership communication fosters deeper connections, builds trust, and drives creativity and innovation. It is particularly essential during periods of change or disruption, as communication is one of the three critical competencies for successful change leadership, according to research.

4.1.2 The Connection Between Communication, Conversations, and Culture

In organizations, conversations form the foundation of most communication. Daily interactions—both formal and informal—between colleagues and leaders shape the workplace environment. The more effective these conversations are, the stronger the organization becomes, as meaningful dialogue fosters a positive and resilient culture.

4.1.3 Core Traits of Effective Leadership Communication

- **Authenticity:** Be honest and sincere. Communicate in your voice, avoiding corporate jargon or forced eloquence. Let your personality, background, and values shine through. People respect and follow authentic leaders who stay true to themselves.
- **Accessibility:** Visibility is a powerful form of communication. Effective leaders don't just rely on emails and official messages—they are present, approachable, and engaged. Consistently showing up and interacting with employees, especially during crises, strengthens leadership impact.
- **Clarity & Confidence:** Clear and confident communication prevents ambiguity and misinterpretation. Speak with specificity, reinforce your words with nonverbal cues, and communicate not just with facts but also with emotions and values. Clarity and confidence build trust and commitment within a team.
- **Empathy & Respect:** Empathy is a crucial leadership trait, especially in communication. Employees appreciate leaders who acknowledge their concerns and challenges. By listening actively and addressing their feelings, leaders foster a culture of psychological safety, where employees feel valued and heard.

- **Trust:** Trust cannot be mandated; it must be earned through consistent and transparent communication. Leaders who model integrity and openness encourage authenticity within their teams. A culture of trust empowers employees to share ideas, take risks, and drive innovation.

By mastering these core traits, leaders can enhance their communication effectiveness, build stronger relationships, and create a workplace culture that thrives on trust and collaboration.

4.1.4 The High Cost of Poor Leadership Communication

Workplace communication is constantly evolving. Leaders must continuously seek new ways to make their communication more effective, purposeful, and trustworthy. But what happens when communication becomes stagnant, disorganized, or unclear?

Leaders may unintentionally undermine their efforts to improve communication. They might withhold information out of fear of oversharing, speak impulsively at the wrong moment, or be overly blunt with a colleague.

These challenges often arise in high-stress situations—when expectations or deadlines aren't met, when opportunities are lost, or when innovation is lacking. While this can be frustrating, it's crucial to address conflicts directly through open conversations and constructive discussions. When conflicts are mismanaged, costs continue to rise—whether in the form of tangible expenses like employee turnover or intangible losses such as low morale, poor decision-making, and broken trust.

4.1.5 Effective Communication: Barriers and Strategies

1. **Listening**

Barriers to Active Listening

- Focusing on a personal agenda – When we spend our listening time formulating our next response, we fail to fully engage with what the speaker is saying.
- Experiencing information overload – Too much information or stimulation can make it difficult to focus. Try to concentrate on relevant details and the key points being conveyed.
- Criticizing the speaker – Avoid getting distracted by judgments about the speaker's style or delivery. Focus on their message rather than the messenger.
- Being distracted by strong emotional responses – If you experience a strong emotional reaction, acknowledge it but refocus on listening. Make a conscious effort not to get lost in your emotions.
- Getting distracted by external "noise" – Audible distractions, such as phone notifications or background conversations, can interfere with listening. Minimize

controllable noise by silencing devices and choosing a quiet environment when possible. Figurative distractions, like uncomfortable room conditions or inappropriate decor, can also impact attention.

- Experiencing physical illness or pain – If you're unwell or in pain, it may be difficult to listen effectively. Communicate your situation and, if necessary, reschedule the conversation.

Strategies for Active Listening

Active listening involves fully understanding the speaker's message while demonstrating interest and engagement.

- Stop – Focus entirely on the speaker's thoughts and feelings. Quiet your internal dialogue and shift your attention to their message.
- Look – Observe nonverbal cues such as body language and facial expressions, which can add depth to the conversation. Active listeners show engagement through eye contact and positive body language.
- Listen – Absorb the key details and central ideas rather than focusing on individual words. Seek an overall understanding of the speaker's intent.
- Be empathetic – Put yourself in the speaker's position to better understand their emotions. Maintain a calm and composed presence while acknowledging their perspective.
- Ask questions – Clarify your understanding and demonstrate engagement by asking relevant questions.
- Paraphrase – If you don't have specific questions, restate the speaker's main points in your own words to confirm understanding. This allows the speaker to clarify or elaborate if needed.

2. Perception

Barriers to Accurate Perception

- Stereotyping and generalizing – Avoid forming conclusions based on limited experiences or preconceptions. Keep an open mind and assess situations individually.
- Not investing time – Jumping to conclusions without gathering enough information can lead to misconceptions. Take the time to understand the full context.
- Negativity bias – Many people tend to focus more on the negative aspects of a situation, allowing one negative comment to outweigh multiple positive ones. Strive for a balanced perspective.
- Assuming similar interpretations – Different individuals may perceive the same situation in different ways. Confirm mutual understanding by checking interpretations with others.
- Experiencing incongruent cues – Verbal and nonverbal messages should align. If someone's body language contradicts their words, seek clarification to avoid misinterpretation.

Strategies for Accurate Perception

- Analyze your perceptions – Regularly question how your perceptions are formed. Seek feedback from others and ensure you're not making unwarranted assumptions.
- Work on improving perception – Recognize your personal biases and work to overcome them. Check-in with yourself and others to refine your understanding.
- Focus on others – Develop your ability to understand people by actively listening, gathering relevant information, and considering different perspectives.

3. Verbal Communication

Barriers to Effective Verbal Communication

- Lacking clarity – Avoid overly abstract, formal, or jargon-heavy language, as it can obscure your message rather than enhance it.
- Using stereotypes and generalizations – Making sweeping statements reduces credibility and can lead to misunderstandings. Be mindful of complexity and avoid polarizing language.
- Jumping to conclusions – Do not assume you know the reasoning behind events or automatically attach meaning to certain facts. Gather sufficient information before making inferences.
- Dysfunctional responses – Ignoring a comment, responding irrelevantly, or frequently interrupting disrupts effective communication and discourages genuine dialogue.
- Lacking confidence – Low self-confidence, shyness, or difficulty being assertive can hinder clear communication. Understanding your rights and value in a conversation can help you express yourself effectively.

Strategies for Effective Verbal Communication

- Focus on the issue, not the person – Avoid personalizing discussions. Express concerns about the task or situation rather than making it about individuals.
- Be genuine – Communicate honestly and openly while maintaining integrity in your interactions.
- Empathize rather than remain detached – While maintaining professional boundaries, show care and sensitivity toward colleagues to foster strong working relationships.
- Be flexible towards others – Remain open to different perspectives and approaches. Embracing diversity leads to creativity and innovation.
- Value yourself and your experiences – Stand firm in expressing your thoughts and ideas. When you undervalue yourself, others may do the same.
- Use affirming responses – Acknowledge others' experiences and contributions. Show appreciation, ask questions, provide feedback, and validate their perspectives, even when you disagree.

SUMMARY

Effective communication is a key leadership skill that helps leaders inspire, guide, and build trust within their teams. Strong leaders communicate with clarity, actively listen, and adapt their messaging to different audiences. They use both verbal and nonverbal cues effectively, provide constructive feedback, and resolve conflicts to maintain a positive work environment. Transparency and emotional intelligence foster trust and engagement, while strong communication during crises ensures stability and direction. By mastering these skills, leaders enhance collaboration, boost morale, and drive organizational success.

EXERCISES:

1. Why is communication important for leaders?
2. How does effective communication contribute to leadership success?
3. What are the common barriers to leadership communication?
4. Why is transparency important in leadership communication?
5. What strategies can leaders use to improve their perception accuracy?
6. What are the consequences of mismanaged communication during conflicts?
7. How does communication drive innovation and creativity within teams?

www.ingramcontent.com/pod-product-compliance
Lightning Source LLC
LaVergne TN
LVHW070944160826
845679LV00022B/1907